THE CONFIDENCE COMPASS ADVENTURES

Book 1

The Confidence Compass Adventures

The LION of BELONGING

A magical story about kindness, courage, and discovering where confidence begins.

TANYA BOOKE

Dedication

For **Sophia and Ella** —
my two North Stars, my greatest joy, and the bright little lights behind every
page of this book. You are the reason this story exists.
You are the reason I believe courage can be gentle, kindness can be powerful,
and confidence can grow one small brave moment at a time. Thank you for
filling my world with wonder, big questions, wild ideas, belly laughs, deep
feelings, and the kind of love that changes a person forever.
You remind me every day that the real magic is not in being perfect — it's in
being curious, brave, loving, and wonderfully yourself.

Preface

From My North to Yours

When I was a kid, confidence didn't come naturally to me.

I wasn't the loudest in the room.
I didn't always raise my hand.
And trying something new? That felt big. Sometimes too big.

But something shifted for me when I started playing sports.

It wasn't about being the best.
It was about trying.
Falling.
Getting back up.
And realizing—little by little—that confidence wasn't something you were born
with...

It was something you could build.

That idea stayed with me as I grew up.

Even as an adult—through school, work, and life—I realized that confidence isn't one big thing. It's made up of smaller skills. Things we can practice. Things we can learn.

That's where the idea for the **Confidence Compass** came from.

A simple way to help kids understand:

- what confidence actually *is*

- how it shows up

- and how to find their way back to it when they feel unsure

I created this story because I believe every child deserves to feel:

- brave enough to try

- safe enough to be themselves

- and strong enough to keep going

Even when things feel a little scary.

This book is for the quiet kids.
The bold kids.

The "not sure yet" kids.

And maybe... a little bit for the grown-ups, too.

Because confidence isn't something we finish learning.

It's something we practice—together.

—Tanya

What to Expect in This Color-Reading Book

This isn't just a story—it's something you and your child can *experience together.*

As you read, you'll notice a few special things woven throughout the book:

Bold Words
Certain words are highlighted in bold. These connect to a simple glossary at the end of the book to help you and your child learn the language of confidence together.

Try-It Moments
You'll find small, fun actions you can pause and try—helping bring the story to life in real ways.

Coloring Pages
At the end of the book, there are coloring pages inspired by the story—designed to reinforce key ideas while giving kids space to reflect and create.

The Confidence Compass
Throughout the journey, you'll begin to recognize the different parts of confidence—and how your child can use them in their everyday life.

This book is meant to be read, colored, talked about, and lived.

So take your time.

Pause when something feels meaningful.
Laugh. Try things. Be a little silly.

Because confidence doesn't grow from perfection—

It grows from practice.

Contents

1. The Night the Compass Appeared   1
The First Step North

2. The Lion of Belonging   15
The Heart of the Compass

3. The Lion's Lesson   32
Belonging Starts With You

4. The First Direction   48
Practicing the Heart of the Compass

5. A Different Kind of Brave   61
When You're Still Scared... and You Try Anyway

6. The Beginning Inside You   80
What Confidence Really Means

What Belonging Really Means 87
The Lion of Belonging™ Playbook

A Sneak Peek… 97
The Confidence Compass Adventures Book 2: The Wolf of Courage

Glossary 103

Let's Color! 111
The Lion of Belonging Coloring Book

The Night the Compass Appeared

Sophia and Ella were not supposed to be outside.

Not when it was getting dark.
Not in the backyard.
And definitely not chasing Rupert.

But Rupert had never been particularly interested in rules.

Rupert was a one-year-old terrier with three very serious hobbies:

barking at absolutely nothing,
digging holes like he was searching for treasure,

and running away at exactly the worst possible moment.

Which is exactly what he was doing now.

"RUUUUPERT!"

Sophia's voice rang out across the yard, sharp and urgent—but it was too late.
He was already gone.

A streak of scruffy fur.
A blur of paws.
A flash of total chaos.
And then... nothing.
He disappeared straight into the trees at the edge of the yard,
like the shadows had swallowed him whole.

Ella didn't look worried.
She looked... delighted.
"This," she said, grinning, "is how every great adventure starts."
Sophia shot her a look. "This *adventure* is how we get in trouble."
"Same thing," Ella said cheerfully.
Sophia hesitated.
Just for a second.

She looked back at the house.
The lights were still on.
Everything felt normal back there.
Safe.
Predictable.
Very much *not* full of runaway dogs.
Then she looked at the trees.

Dark.
Quiet.
Mysterious.

And Rupert... was in there.

"Well," Sophia said, taking a breath, "we can't just leave him."

She pushed open the gate.

Ella didn't even wait—

she darted through ahead of her.

Alongside Ella, was Chloe.

Chloe was also a terrier, but that was where the similarities ended.
Rupert was powered almost entirely by bad ideas.
Chloe was ten, wiser, calmer, and absolutely not impressed.
She trotted along, with the look of a dog who had seen Rupert do something
ridiculous many, many times before.
Which, honestly...
she had.
She gave one little huff through her nose and kept going—
not as wild as Rupert,
but with just enough spunk to say she was still very much part of the mission.

The woods weren't very big.

Just a small stretch of trees tucked behind the yard.
The kind of place where squirrels held what looked like very important meetings...
and birds argued loudly about snacks.
But tonight...
something was different.
The air felt still.
Too still.
And then—
Ella stopped.
"Do you see that?" she whispered.
Sophia looked.
At first, she didn't see anything.
Just shadows and branches and patches of dark grass.
And then—
There it was.
A glow.

Soft.
Golden.
Flickering gently, like it was breathing.
Not bright like a flashlight.
Not sharp like a star.
Warmer than that.

Alive, somehow.
They stepped closer.
Carefully.
Quietly.
Even Chloe slowed down now.
In a small clearing, right in the middle of the trees...
was something none of them had ever seen before.
A stone compass.
It was wide—about the size of a dinner plate—resting flat in the grass as if it
had always been there.
But it hadn't.
Sophia would have noticed.
She was sure of it.
The stone was smooth, almost worn, like it had been touched a thousand times.
Carved into it were faint lines stretching outward—north, south, east,
west—but not in the way a normal compass looked.
These lines felt... different.
Like they meant something more.
At the very center...was a star.
And that's where the glow was coming from.
It didn't shine. It pulsed.
Soft and steady. Like a heartbeat.

"Um…" Ella whispered, suddenly less bold than before. "Was that always here?"

Sophia shook her head slowly.

"No," she said.

Her voice came out quieter than she expected.

She crouched down beside it.

The air felt warmer near the stone.

Not hot.

Just… safe.

Comforting.

Like standing in sunlight after being cold.

Sophia reached her hand toward it—then paused.

Behind her, Chloe gave a low little huff and tilted her head, as if she had some very serious questions about all of this.

Ella glanced at her and whispered, "See? Even Chloe thinks this is weird."

Chloe stepped closer, sniffed once, then took one careful step back.

That was not exactly a yes.

Sophia gave a tiny smile.
"Things are already weird."
And then—
very gently—
she placed her fingers on the glowing star.
The moment she touched it...
the light shifted.
The lines on the stone began to glow, one by one, stretching outward like golden
paths.
And somewhere, deep in the trees—
there was a sound.
A soft rustle.
Then another.
Like something...
or someone...
had just woken up.

The Lion of Belonging

THE HEART OF THE COMPASS

Around the edge of the stone compass were five symbols.

Not letters.

Not numbers.

Shapes.

Simple... but somehow important.

Sophia leaned closer.

"*There*," she said, pointing. "*Look*."

A heart.

A square.

A triangle.

A star.

And a diamond.

Each one carved carefully into the stone, like they had been placed there on purpose.

Like they were waiting.

"For what?" Ella whispered.

Sophia didn't answer. She didn't know. But she could feel it.

This wasn't just a rock.

Ella slowly reached out, her fingers hovering just above the compass.

"I don't know..." she whispered.

The glow at the center flickered softly, almost as if it were listening.

Watching.

Waiting.

Ella glanced at Sophia.

Sophia gave her a small, steady nod.

"Okay," Ella said.

Very gently... she placed her hand on the compass.

Nothing happened.

Not at first.

One second.

Two.

Three—

Rupert bounded forward and plopped his paw right on top.

"RUFF!"

Chloe tilted her head, watching closely.

Then she seemed to think, *Well, if Rupert's doing it... I better help too.*

So she stepped forward and placed her paw beside his.

Now all four adventurers—hands and paws—were touching the compass.

And then—

everything changed.

A voice filled the clearing.

Soft.

Deep.

Not loud—but everywhere.

Like wind moving through tall grass.

"Welcome."

Ella jumped back. "WHO SAID THAT?!"

Sophia spun around. "Did you hear that?!"

Chloe froze.

Even Rupert stopped moving.

The trees seemed to shift.

Not moving exactly...

but leaning in.

Listening.

The golden light stretched across the ground, longer now, brighter.

And from the shadows between the trees...

something stepped forward.

At first, all they saw were eyes.

Warm.

Steady.

Glowing faintly like the compass.

Then—a shape.

Large.

Powerful.

Moving slowly, carefully, like it didn't want to scare them.

A lion.

Not like the ones in books. Not like the ones at the zoo.

Bigger. **Stronger**. But also…somehow…**kind**.

His fur shimmered softly in the golden light.

His eyes weren't fierce.

They were calm.

Understanding.

Like he already knew them.

"Don't worry," the lion said, his voice gentle and warm.

"I'm a friendly lion."

Rupert barked immediately, tail wagging like this was the best day of his life.

Sophia blinked.

"A... talking... lion?"

The lion smiled.

"Yes."

Ella looked at Sophia.
"Okay, so this is happening."

Sophia nodded slowly.

"This is definitely happening."

The lion chuckled softly.

He stepped closer to the compass.

The light shifted again, glowing brighter beneath his paws.

"This," he said, "is the Confidence Compass."

The word seemed to settle in the air.

Confidence.

Sophia leaned forward.

"The... *compass*?"

The lion nodded.

"It helps you find something very important."

"What?" Ella asked.

The lion looked at her, then at Sophia.

"Yourself."

He gently lifted one large paw and pointed to the glowing center.

The heart. It pulsed softly beneath his touch.

"This," he said, "is where it begins."

Sophia leaned in closer.

"The heart?"

The lion nodded again.

"Belonging."

Ella frowned slightly. "Belonging?"

The word felt... simple. But also... not simple at all.

The lion's voice softened.

"Most people think confidence starts with being brave."

Ella nodded quickly. "Yeah. Like doing scary things."

"Or not being afraid," Sophia added.

The lion shook his head.

"No."

The word was gentle.

But clear.

"Confidence does not begin with bravery."

The girls looked at each other.

"It doesn't?" Ella asked.

"No," the lion said.

He sat down beside the compass, calm and steady.
"Confidence begins long before that."
He placed his paw over the glowing heart again.
"It begins when you feel something deep inside you."
He looked at them, one at a time.
Slowly.
Kindly.

He spoke again, softer now.
"It begins when you know…three things"
He raised his paw:

"first, that **I belong**."

The heart glowed brighter.

"second that, **I matter**."

The light spread outward.

"And third, that **I can be myself**."

The clearing felt warmer. Safer. Like the whole world had just taken a deep breath.

Sophia didn't realize she had leaned in closer.
But she had.
"What if…" she started, then hesitated.
"What if you don't feel that way?"
The lion looked at her.
Not surprised.
Not worried.
Just… understanding.
"That," he said gently,
"is why you're here."

The Lion's Lesson

BELONGING STARTS WITH YOU

Sophia looked down, twisting a small leaf between her fingers.

She didn't look at the lion.

She didn't look at Ella.

She just watched the leaf bend and fold.

"Sometimes…" she said quietly,

"I don't feel like I belong."

The words felt heavy once they were out.

Like they had been sitting inside her for a long time.

The lion didn't rush.

He didn't interrupt.

He didn't say, *"That's not true."*

He simply listened.

"Tell me," he said gently.

Sophia swallowed.
"At school…"
She paused.
The words were harder to say out loud.

"Everyone already has someone."
She looked up just for a second, then back down again.
"They sit together... talk together... walk together..."
Her voice grew smaller.
"And I don't know where to go."
The clearing went quiet.
Even the trees seemed to hold still.
The lion nodded slowly.
"That feeling..."
He paused, choosing his words carefully.
"...is very common."
Sophia looked up, surprised.
"It is?"
The lion gave a small, knowing smile.
"Even lions feel it sometimes."
Ella blinked. "Wait... really?"
The lion chuckled softly.
"Yes. Even in a pride, there are moments when you wonder...
...*Where do I fit?*"
He leaned closer to Sophia, his voice warm and steady—
like a blanket on a cold night.
"Belonging is not something you wait for."
The heart on the compass glowed a little brighter.
Sophia frowned slightly.

"What do you mean?"

The lion lifted his paw and gently tapped the glowing heart.

"Most people think belonging is something *someone else* gives you."

"An invitation."

"A seat."

"A group that says, 'You can come here.'"

Sophia nodded slowly.

"Yeah…"

"But *belonging*," the lion continued,

"also **grows** when you give it."

Sophia blinked.

"*Give it?*"

He nodded.

"When you **include** someone…"

"When you **smile** first…"

"When you **sit beside** someone who is also alone…"

"You are **creating belonging**."

The light from the compass stretched outward again, soft and golden.

Sophia thought about that.
"So helping someone else... helps *you*?"
The lion smiled.
"Belonging grows in both directions."
Sophia hesitated.
"What if..."
she said slowly,
"...I feel nervous?"
The lion nodded immediately.
"Of course you will."
He leaned in just a little closer.
"Bravery does not mean the fear goes away."
Sophia looked up at him.
His eyes were calm.
Certain.
"It means you choose kindness..."
He paused.
"...anyway."

Right then—
Rupert noticed something extremely important.

The lion's tail.

Fluffy and slowly swishing.

Absolutely irresistible.

Rupert froze. Lowered himself to the ground.

Wiggled his back end like a tiny, determined hunter.

Chloe watched from behind.

Still.

Silent.

Already knowing exactly what was about to happen.

And then—Rupert LAUNCHED.
"RUUUPERT!" Sophia shouted.
The lion lifted his tail just in time.
Rupert flew past it—rolled across the grass—and popped back up like nothing
had happened.
Ella burst into laughter.
"Did you see that?!"

Chloe sat down, gave a long, slow blink…
and then turned her head slightly away.
As if to say:
I do not know this dog.
The lion exhaled, amused.
"We appear to have a… spirited companion."
Rupert barked proudly.

The lion stood again and turned back to the compass.
"The compass has many directions," he said.
The other symbols began to glow softly now.
He pointed to each one as he spoke.
"The **Wolf** teaches **courage**…"
"…the kind that keeps going, even when things are hard."
"The **Owl** teaches you to **understand** your feelings…"
"…instead of being overwhelmed by them."
"The **Dragon** teaches you to use your **voice**…"
"…even when it feels scary."
"And the **Phoenix**…"
He paused.
The light flickered gently.
"…teaches you how to **rise again**."
Ella's eyes widened.
"Wait… we get to meet them?"
The lion's smile held something quiet.
Something knowing.
"If you follow the compass…"
He looked at each of them.
"…you will find them when you need them."

Sophia looked back down at the heart.
Still glowing.
Still steady.
Still warm.
"What if I forget?" she asked softly.
The lion's voice was gentle.
"You won't."
He tapped the compass once more.
"Because it isn't just here."
He looked at her.
Right at her.
"It's already in you."
The clearing grew still again.
The light softened.
And somewhere, just beyond the trees...
something moved.
Waiting.

The First Direction

PRACTICING THE HEART OF THE COMPASS

The next morning at school, the playground was loud and busy.

Kids raced across the blacktop.

Jump ropes slapped against the pavement.

A soccer ball rolled through the grass, chased by a pack of shouting players.

Laughter bounced through the air like it had somewhere important to be.

Sophia stood at the edge for a moment.

Just watching.

The noise.

The movement.

The groups already formed.

She shifted her backpack higher on her shoulder.

And then—she saw her.

A girl sitting alone on a bench.

Quiet.

Still.

Looking down at her shoes like they were the most interesting thing in the world.

Sophia felt it right away.

That familiar little knot in her chest.

The not-knowing.

The wondering.

The quiet swirl of questions that showed up before she even realized it.

Should I go over?
What if she doesn't want to talk?
What if I say something weird?
What if she already has friends and I just don't know it?

Sophia shifted her weight.

One step forward.

Then stopped.

That tiny voice crept in again.

What if she doesn't want you there?

Sophia glanced back at the playground.

Everyone else looked busy.

Connected.

Sure of where they belonged.

Then—

she remembered the lion.

Not just what he said.

But how it felt.

Warm.

Steady.

True.

Belonging begins with one small, brave moment.

Sophia took a breath.

Not a big, dramatic one.

Just enough.

And then—

she walked over.

"Hi," she said softly.

The girl looked up, surprised. Like she hadn't expected anyone to stop.

"Hi," she said back.

Sophia gave a small smile.

"I'm Sophia."

The girl tucked a piece of hair behind her ear.

"I'm Maya."

For a second, neither of them said anything.

The playground noise filled the space between them.

Then Sophia nodded toward the other kids.

"Do you want to play with me?"

Maya blinked.

"Really?"

There was something in her voice. Not disbelief exactly. Just... hope that wasn't sure it should be there.

"Really," Sophia said.

Simple. Clear. **True**.

And right then—

something changed.

Maya's face softened.

Like a tiny light had turned on behind her eyes.

"Okay," she said, smiling now.

They stood up together.

Not rushed.

Not awkward.

Just... together.

And as they ran toward the other kids—
the bench didn't feel quite so lonely anymore.
As they joined the game, Sophia felt something shift inside her.
Warm.
Quiet.
Almost like the glow from the compass.
It wasn't loud.
It wasn't a big, cheering kind of feeling.
No one clapped.
No one pointed.
No one said, *"Wow, that was amazing."*

But Sophia noticed.

Because something inside her had changed.

Just a little.

Like a small light had been switched on in a place that used to feel unsure.

She had helped someone else feel less alone.

And somehow...

she felt less alone too.

That feeling stayed with her.
Through the rest of the day.

Through math class.

Through lunch.

Through the final bell ringing.

It stayed with her on the walk home.

Through dinner.

Through bath time.

Through the soft rustle of pajamas.

And the quiet, sleepy hush that comes when a day is almost done.

Later that night, as Sophia looked up at the stars,
she placed her hand over her heart.
Just for a moment.
She could still feel it.
That small, steady warmth.
Not gone.
Not fading.
Still there.

The kind of brave that doesn't shout.
The kind that doesn't stomp or sparkle.
The kind that starts as a whisper...
and grows.
Slowly.
Softly.
Deep inside you.
And once it begins—
it doesn't like to disappear.

A Different Kind of Brave

WHEN YOU'RE STILL SCARED... AND YOU TRY ANYWAY

Later that night, when the house had grown still...

and the stars began to scatter across the sky...

Sophia felt it again.

That same gentle pull.

That warm, familiar flutter in her chest.

Not loud.

Not urgent.

But steady.

Like something quietly calling her back.

She sat up in bed.
Listened.
The house was silent.
Soft breathing down the hall.
A distant hum.
Everything normal.
And yet...
not.

Sophia slipped out of bed and padded quietly across the floor.
By the time she reached the hallway—

Ella was already there.

Wide awake.

Waiting.

"You felt it too?" Sophia whispered.

Ella nodded immediately.

"Yeah."

She placed a hand lightly over her chest.

"It's like... something is pulling me."

Sophia smiled a little.

"Me too."

They didn't need to say anything else.

They already knew.

Outside, the night air was cool and soft.

The grass whispered beneath their feet as they made their way toward the trees.

Rupert didn't need to be told.

He burst ahead of them, racing through the yard like this was his favorite kind of mission.

Chloe followed behind at her usual pace—

steady, quiet, completely unbothered—

though she gave Rupert a long look that clearly said:

This again.

The trees opened into the clearing.

And there it was.

The compass.

Waiting.

Sophia stepped forward first.

Slower this time.

More certain.

She knelt beside the stone and placed her hand gently on its surface.

Warm.
Steady.
Safe.
Like it recognized her.
Like it had been expecting her.
Sophia watched, a small smile forming.
"I think it's still working."
Ella let out a breath she didn't realize she'd been holding.
"Good," she said quietly.
Because something inside her already knew—
something was about to happen.
The compass responded.

Its glow deepened.
Brightened.
Soft golden light spilled across the ground, stretching into the trees—
like the moon had tipped sideways just to watch.
Fireflies drifted into the clearing, rising and falling like tiny floating lanterns.
The air changed.

Not louder.

Not colder.

Just... different.

Still.

Charged.

Waiting.

Then—

just ahead—

something moved.

A shape.

Gray.

Silent.

The girls stood.

Looked up.

And stepped out from the shadows—

he appeared.

A wolf.

He did not rush.

He did not growl.

He did not try to be anything other than what he was.

Still.

Grounded.

Unshaken.

He stood there, watching them with steady, knowing eyes.

Ella's breath caught.

Her heart began to beat faster—

loud enough she thought he might hear it.

Sophia didn't step back.

But she didn't step forward either.

She simply stood.

Watching.

There was something about him.

Not loud.

Not fierce in the way she expected.

But strong.

Steady.

Certain.

Safe.

The wolf took one step forward.

Then another.

The compass in Sophia's hand pulsed softly.

Glow...

pause...

glow.

Sophia leaned in just slightly.

"He's not here to scare us," she whispered.

Ella nodded, even though her fingers curled tightly against her palm.

"I know," she whispered back.

"...I'm just a little scared anyway."

Sophia gave a small smile.

"Me too."

The wolf stopped just a few steps away.

Close enough now that they could see him clearly—

the quiet power in him.

The way he held himself without needing to prove anything.

The way he didn't rush them.

Didn't push.

Didn't demand.

He simply...

was.

"I think..." Ella said slowly,

"...he's here to help us."

The wolf tilted his head.
Not as a question.
But as if he understood.
He stepped closer.
Slow.
Calm.
Until he stood beside them in the moonlit grass.
His thick fur held the warmth of the night.
And somehow—just being near him made the girls feel warmer too.
Safer.
Steadier.
Like the fear inside them didn't have to disappear...
for them to stay.
The wolf leaned his head near theirs.
Not bowing.

Not shrinking.

Just... meeting them where they were.

And in that quiet moment—

they understood.

Courage was not loud.

Courage was this.

Standing.

Breathing.

Staying.

Even when your heart beat a little faster.

Even when your hands felt unsure.

"You don't have to be fearless..." Sophia whispered.

Ella looked at her.

Then back at the wolf.

"...to be brave."

The wolf's eyes softened.

As if to say—

Exactly.

Behind them,

Rupert attempted to pounce on a firefly and completely missed.

He tumbled sideways into the grass.

Chloe closed her eyes briefly.

As if gathering patience from another dimension.

The compass pulsed again.

Stronger this time.

And somewhere, deep inside Sophia—

something shifted.

The kind of strength that doesn't rush.

The kind that stays.
The kind that says—
I can try.
And this time...
she believed it.

The Beginning Inside You

WHAT CONFIDENCE REALLY MEANS

The Wolf of Courage had arrived.

And that is how Sophia and Ella learned something important.

Confidence does not begin
when you are the loudest,
or the boldest,
or the one who never feels afraid.
It begins somewhere quieter.
Somewhere deeper.
It begins when you know—
in your heart—

I belong.
I matter.
I am safe to be myself.
And even then...

there will be moments
when your voice feels small,
your hands feel shaky,
your heart beats just a little too fast.

Moments when being yourself feels hard.
Moments when courage feels far away.
And that's when confidence asks for something more.
Not perfection. Not fearlessness. **Courage**.

The kind that steps forward gently
into the unknown.
The kind that doesn't rush. The kind that stays.
The kind that whispers—

you can do this...

even now.

The clearing grew quiet again.

The fireflies drifted higher,
fading into the dark sky like tiny stars finding their place.
And somehow—

without saying a word—

they both knew.

They didn't have to wait
to feel confident.

They didn't have to become
someone else.

They didn't have to be fearless
to begin.
They had already started.

What Belonging Really Means

BELONGING IS NOT ABOUT fitting in.
It's not about being liked by everyone.
It's not about avoiding conflict.

Belonging is the deep, internal feeling of:

I am safe.
I am accepted.
I matter here.

When a child feels belonging, confidence grows naturally.

When they don't, something else takes over.

They begin to:

- shrink

- overperform

- people-please

- or act out

Behavior is often a signal—**not the problem.**

The Lion Layer (Esteem)

The Lion represents **Esteem**—the foundation of confidence.

This is where a child learns:

I matter, even when I mess up.
I am loved, even when I struggle.
I belong, just as I am.

Without this layer, everything else feels shaky.

Before teaching skills...
Before correcting behavior...

Build the Lion.

The Hidden Trap

Most of us don't mean to—but we accidentally tie belonging to behavior.

It sounds like:

- praise only when they succeed

- extra warmth when they behave well

- distance when they struggle

And children quietly learn:

I belong when I'm good.

But what we want them to know is:

I belong no matter what.

Behavior can be corrected.
Belonging should never be at risk.

Belonging Lives in Language

Small shifts in what we say create big shifts in how children feel.

Instead of:
"I'm proud of you."
Try adding:
"I love who you are."

Instead of:
"Good job winning!"
Try:
"I loved watching you try."

Instead of:
"Why would you do that?"
Try:
"Help me understand what happened."

Instead of:
"Stop crying."
Try:

"You're allowed to feel this."

The 3 Daily Belonging Deposits

Think of belonging like a bank account.

It grows through small, consistent deposits:

1. Eye Contact + Presence
"I see you."

2. Physical Connection
A hug, a hand squeeze, sitting close

3. Specific Words
"I love being your mom."
"I'm so glad you're you."

These moments may feel small—
but they build emotional security over time.

When Your Child Feels Left Out

This is one of the biggest threats to belonging.

Our instinct is to fix it quickly.

But connection comes first.

Start with:
"That really hurts."

Then ask:
"What do you need right now—comfort or help?"

Later, you can guide:
"What's one small step you could take next time?"

Belonging first.
Problem-solving second.

The "Stay Close" Rule

When kids struggle, they often expect distance.

That's when they need closeness the most.

If your child:

- lashes out

- shuts down

- pushes you away

Your job is simple (not easy):

Stay close.

Not to fix.
Not to lecture.

Just to show:
I'm not going anywhere.

Repair Is Powerful

You will mess up.

We all do.

What matters most is what happens after.

Say:
"Hey... I didn't handle that well."
"I'm sorry."
"You still matter to me."

This teaches your child something critical:

Belonging is stronger than mistakes.

Building Belonging at Home

Belonging isn't built in big speeches.

It's built in repeated moments.

Create small rituals:

- Friday night movie

- "High/Low" at dinner

- a secret handshake

- a morning hug before school

These moments say:

This is your safe place.

The Confidence Kid Starts Here

Before confidence...
Before courage...
Before voice...

There is belonging.

A confident child is not created by pushing harder.

They are built by knowing:

✔ I am safe
✔ I am loved
✔ I matter

The Lion comes first.

Always.

For You, the Parent

You don't have to be perfect to create belonging.

You just have to be:

- present

- willing

- human

Your child doesn't need a perfect parent.

They need a connected one.

Your Child's North Begins Here

Belonging is the starting point.

It's the root.
It's the anchor.
It's the reason your child will:

- try again

- speak up

- take risks

- become who they are meant to be

When in doubt...

Come back to the Lion.

A Sneak Peek...

The Confidence Compass Adventures Book 2: The Wolf of Courage

Sophia held the compass a little tighter.

The golden light flickered softly.

The wolf stood just ahead.

Still.
Quiet.
Watching.

Ella whispered,
"He's different."

Sophia nodded.

The lion had felt warm.

The wolf felt... steady.

The wolf took one slow step forward.

"Are you ready," he asked,
"for the next step?"

Sophia looked down at the compass.

The heart still glowed.

But now...

another symbol shimmered.

A square.

"What does that mean?" she asked.

The wolf's voice was calm.

"That," he said,
"is where trying begins."

Ella frowned.

"Trying?"

The wolf nodded.

"Yes."

Sophia hesitated.

"What if something is hard?"

The wolf tilted his head.

"It will be."

Ella crossed her arms.

"What if we can't do it?"

The wolf's eyes were kind.

"You won't."

He paused.

"Not at first."

Sophia blinked.

"That doesn't sound very helpful."

The wolf stepped closer.

"It is the most helpful thing of all."

He turned and looked down a narrow path just beyond the clearing.

It hadn't been there before.

Dark.

Quiet.

Uncertain.

"Come," he said.

Sophia and Ella looked at each other.

Then back at the path.

Then—

they took one small step forward.

And that is how they began to learn something new:

Confidence does not grow
when everything is easy.

Confidence grows
the moment you try.

And sometimes...

when it feels hard...

when it doesn't work...

when you want to stop—

trying again
is the bravest step of all.

Glossary

1. **Be Yourself:** Being yourself means *being the real you.* You don't try to act like someone else. You share your own thoughts, feelings, and style. You are proud of who you are.

   ○ **Try this:** Wear or draw something that shows what **you** like (your favorite color or a fun design). Remember, it's great to be *you!*

2. **Belonging:** Belonging is the warm feeling that you are *part of a group or family.* You feel accepted and welcome for who you are. You don't feel left out.

   ○ **Try this:** At school, invite a classmate to join your game or sit with you. Help someone else feel like they **belong**, too.

3. **Brave (Bravery):** Being brave means doing something *even if you feel scared.* Bravery doesn't mean you have no fear - it means you try your best **despite** being afraid.

   ○ **Try this:** If something makes you nervous (like speaking in class), take a big breath and **try it once.** Being brave gets easier each time!

4. **Comfort:** Comfort is a feeling of *being safe and feeling better* when you are sad, hurt, or scared. A hug, kind words, or a cozy blanket can give you comfort.

   ○ **Try this:** If you feel upset, hold a favorite toy or talk to someone you love. If a friend is sad, you can gently ask if they want a hug.

5. **Confidence:** Confidence means *believing in yourself.* You feel sure you can **do things** or handle new challenges. Confidence is like a little voice saying, "I can do this."

   ◦ **Try this:** Think of one thing you do well (drawing, reading, riding a bike). When you feel unsure, remember that skill and tell yourself, "I can try!"

6. **Confidence Compass:** The **Confidence Compass** is a special pretend compass in the story that guides Sophia. It glows when she shows confidence. It reminds her of the four big strengths inside her (like **belonging** and **courage**).

   ◦ **Try this:** Draw your own **confidence compass** with four points (for example: *Belonging, Courage, Kindness,* and *Being Yourself*). Each time you do something brave or kind, imagine your compass **lighting up!**

7. **Courage:** Courage is the *inner strength* that helps you do the right thing or try something new **even if it's hard or scary.** It's what makes you brave.

   ◦ **Try this:** Make a **Courage List** of one or two things that feel a little scary (like making a new friend or trying a sport). This week, pick one and **give it a try**, even if you feel nervous.

8. **Encourage**: To encourage means to *give someone support or hope.* When you encourage a person, you cheer them on so they feel brave and keep trying.

   - **Try this:** The next time a friend looks nervous or says "I can't," **smile and say,** "You can do it! I believe in you." Your words can help them feel stronger.

9. **Fear**: Fear is a *strong feeling of being scared.* You might feel fear in your tummy (butterflies) or want to run away. Everyone feels afraid sometimes.

   - **Try this:** Next time you feel **afraid,** talk to a trusted adult or take a few deep breaths. Remember a time you did something even though you were scared - that was you being brave!

10. **Feelings**: Feelings are the *emotions inside us,* like happiness, sadness, anger, or fear. Feelings can be big or small, and they can change. **All feelings are okay.**

   - **Try this:** Each day, **name a feeling** you have (for example, "I feel excited," or "I feel nervous"). You can draw a face that shows that feeling or tell someone about it.

11. **Friendship**: Friendship is a *special bond between people who care about each other.* Friends make each other feel happy, included, and safe.

○ **Try this:** Do something kind for a friend this week. You could draw them a picture, share a snack, or simply say, "I'm glad we're friends!"

12. **Help:** To help means to *do something kind for someone* or make something easier for them. When you help, you show you care.

○ **Try this:** Ask a family member or classmate, "Can I help you with that?" It could be picking up toys, carrying books, or opening a door. Little helps mean a lot!

13. **Include (Included):** To include someone means to *invite them to join* so they are not left out. When you include others, you make them feel part of the group.

○ **Try this:** Look around at recess or lunchtime. If you see someone alone, **ask them to play** or sit with you. Being included can make someone's day brighter!

14. **Kindness:** Kindness means *being caring and thoughtful.* It's doing something nice for others to make them feel good or to help them.

○ **Try this:** Do one **kind** thing today: you could compliment someone ("You did a great job!"), share your toys, or help tidy up without being asked.

15. **Left Out:** Feeling left out is when you think *you're not included* in play or a group. It can make you feel lonely or sad, like you don't belong.

- **Try this:** If you ever feel **left out**, talk to someone you trust about it. And remember to **include others** when you can, so nobody else feels left out.

16. **Lonely**: Feeling lonely means *feeling alone* (like you have no one to play or talk with). Even if people are around, you might feel like nobody sees you.

   - **Try this:** If you feel lonely, try waving or saying **hi** to someone new, or ask, "Can I play too?" If you see someone by themselves, **smile and invite** them to join you.

17. **Matter (Important):** To **matter** means to *be important*. When you say "I matter," it means **you are important just by being you**. You add value to the world and to people's hearts.

   - **Try this:** Every morning, look in the mirror and say, "I **matter** and I am important." Remember that **you** are special to your family and friends, just by being *you*.

18. **Proud**: Feeling proud means you feel *happy and pleased about something good*. You can be proud of yourself or someone else when they do the right thing or work hard.

   - **Try this:** Think of something you did recently (like finishing a tricky homework or helping a friend). Tell yourself, "I'm **proud** I did that!"

Also, if a friend does well, say, "I'm proud of you."

19. **Safe**: Feeling safe means *feeling protected and secure.* You don't feel in danger or scared. Being safe to be yourself means you feel free to show who you really are.

   ○ **Try this:** Think of a place or person that makes you feel **safe** (maybe your room, a cozy reading corner, or a grandparent). If you feel worried, spend time in your safe place or talk to your safe person.

20. **Try Again:** To try again means *to not give up* when something is hard. If something doesn't work the first time, you take a deep breath and **give it another try**.

   ○ **Try this:** When a homework problem or new skill seems tricky, pause and then **try one more time**. Each time you practice, you get a little better - that's the power of trying again!

Let's Color!

THE LION OF BELONGING COLORING BOOK

THE CONFIDENCE COMPASS ADVENTURES
Book 1
The Lion of Belonging
A magical story about kindness, courage, and discovering where confidence begins.
TANYA BOOKE

The
CONFIDENCE
COMPASS
ADVENTURES
The
LION OF BELONGING
BOOK 1
TANYA BOOKE